PENGUIN
MOVES OUT
of the ANTARCTIC

by Nikki Potts • illustrated by Maarten Lenoir

PICTURE WINDOW BOOKS
a capstone imprint

Fish, fish, and more fish!

Penguin is sick of
eating fish.

White, white, and
more white!

Penguin is sick of all the white.

Everything is cold
in the Antarctic.

Everything is hard
and icy. Penguin
wants a change.

ZOOOOM!

Penguin slides into
a soft, sandy paradise.

OUCH!
Sand is not the same as ice!

WHOOSH!

A long-eared jackrabbit darts by.
Look out, Penguin!

Tired and hot,
Penguin looks for
a place to rest.

YIKES!

The chairs here are
a little sharp.

Under a large banana tree,
Penguin finds some shade.

He is not used
to the heat!

Sssssss . . . uddenly,
a snake slithers by.

Penguin wasn't looking
for a new neighbor!

Penguin waddles away as
fast as his flippers can go.

He finds a quiet pond
where he can be alone.

Time for a swim!

Penguin is looking
forward to jumping in.

He has **really** missed water!

PLOP!

But ponds aren't as deep
as the ocean.

Disappointed, Penguin waves
his flippers in the air.

The pond is too shallow.

He can't float.
He can't even get up!

Penguin thinks and thinks.
None of these new places
feel like home.

Where else can he go?

The Arctic!

The Arctic is cold and has plenty of water.

It should be just like Antarctica, right?

Grrrrr!

Or maybe not!
A giant polar bear charges!

Penguin drops to his belly.

He zips to
the ocean
just in
time.

Home at last!

Penguin thinks that maybe his home is pretty nice after all.

It's cold. There is lots of water. He has plenty of friends.

There are no scary snakes or bears!

Welcome home, Penguin!

And the fish aren't
so bad after all.

MORE ABOUT EMPEROR PENGUINS

Although emperor penguins are birds, they can't fly.

Females lay one egg and then leave to hunt. They come back with food after about two months. The male cares for the egg until the chick hatches.

They are the largest penguin species.

Emperor penguins have four layers of waterproof feathers. Feathers help keep the penguins warm.

Strong claws on their feet help emperor penguins move on the slippery ice.

Emperor penguins can eat up to 11 pounds (5 kilograms) of food per day.

ANIMAL PASSPORT

Name: Emperor Penguin

Type: bird

Habitat: Antarctic

Diet: fish

Height: 45 inches
(114.3 centimeters)

Weight: up to 88 pounds
(40 kilograms)

Lifespan: 15 to 20 years

Favorite Activity: belly slides

BOOKS IN THIS SERIES

Habitat Hunter is published by Picture Window Books, an imprint of Capstone.
1710 Roe Crest Drive
North Mankato, Minnesota 56003
www.capstonepub.com

Library of Congress Cataloging-in-Publication Data is available on the Library of Congress website.
ISBN: 978-1-9771-1422-8 (library binding)
ISBN: 978-1-9771-2020-5 (paperback)
ISBN: 978-1-9771-1428-0 (eBook PDF)

Summary: Penguin is bored with its habitat! Follow Penguin as it tries out different places to live. Which habitat will make the best home for Penguin?

Image Credits
Penguin Moves Out of the Antarctic

Shutterstock: BaLL LunLa, 18-19, Denis Belitsky, 21 (bottom), Denis Burdin, 22-23, DonLand, 24-25, evenfh, 2-3, Gaearon Tolon, 26-27, Lorraine Kourafas, 4-5, Mario_Hoppmann, 28-29, Martin Belli, 8-9, Nattapol_Sritogcom, 10-11, Peangdao, 16-17, Phawat, backcover, 14-15, rickyd, 6, Stu Shaw, 21 (top), 31, SUWIT NGAOKAEW, 20-21, ToffeePhoto, 12, 13, TwentyFiveOctober, 7, Vector8DIY, backcover, Wayne Morris, cover

Artistic elements: pingebat, Valeriya_Dor

Editorial Credits
Editor: Mari Bolte; Designer: Kayla Rossow; Media Researcher: Kelly Garvin; Production Specialist: Tori Abraham

All internet sites appearing in back matter were available and accurate when this book was sent to press.